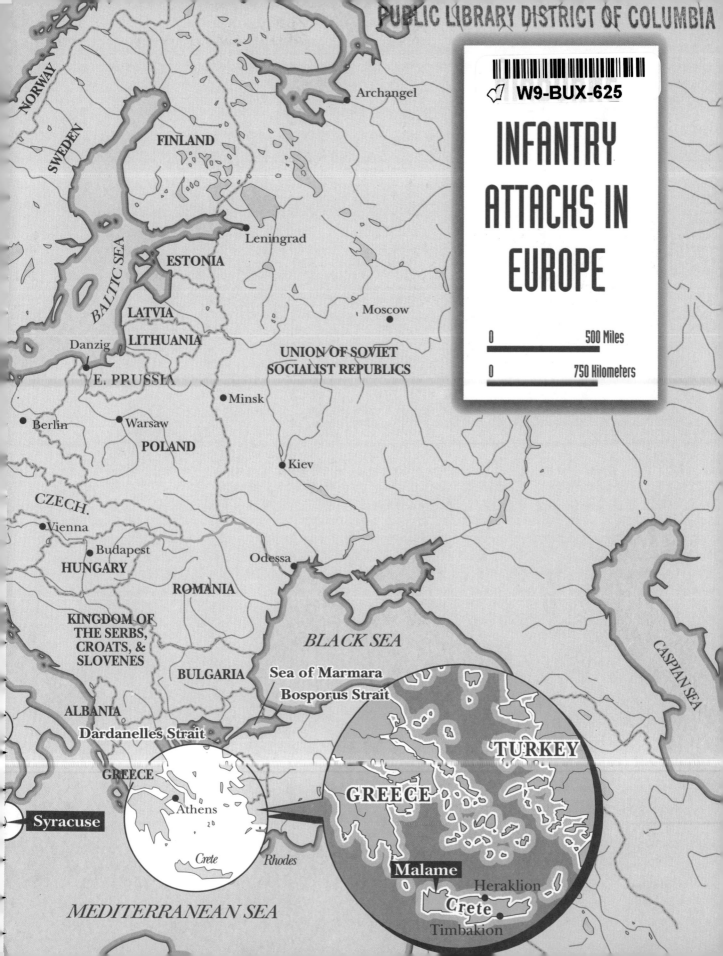

Tom McGowen

ASSAULT FROM THE SKY

AIRBORNE INFANTRY OF WORLD WAR II

TWENTY-FIRST CENTURY BOOKS

Brookfield, Connecticut

Cover photograph courtesy of Bilderdienst Süddeutscher Verlag
Photographs courtesy of Bilderdienst Süddeutscher Verlag: pp. 4, 8, 11, 13, 15, 17, 23, 25, 62; Scala/Art Resource, NY: p. 7; Bildarchiv Preussischer Kulturbesitz: pp. 10, 38, 46; Liaison Agency/Hulton Getty: pp. 18, 35, 41, 50, 53, 56, 61; The Illustrated London News Picture Library: pp. 27, 58; National Archives: p. 29 (#NWDNS-11-SC-194399); UPI/Corbis-Bettmann: p. 31; © Hulton-Deutsch Collection/Corbis: p. 44

Library of Congress Cataloging-in-Publication Data
McGowen, Tom.
Assault from the sky : airborne infantry of World War II / by Tom McGowen.
p. cm. — (Military might)
Includes bibliographical references and index.
ISBN 0-7613-1809-7 (lib. bdg.)
1. World War, 1939-1945—Aerial operations—Juvenile literature. 2. Parachute troops—History—20th century—Juvenile literature. 3. Airborne troops—History—20th century—Juvenile literature. [1. World, War, 1939-1945—Aerial operations. 2. Airborne operations (Military science)] I. Title. II. Series.
D785 .M43 2001
940.54'41—dc21   00-047934

Published by Twenty-First Century Books
A Division of The Millbrook Press, Inc.
2 Old New Milford Road
Brookfield, Connecticut 06804
www.millbrookpress.com

Contents

Chapter 1

SOLDIERS FROM THE SKY

On a quiet spring morning in the Netherlands in 1940, soldiers were on guard throughout the country. The Netherlands was fearful that war might soon break out with its big neighbor, Germany.

Suddenly, soldiers guarding a special bridge began looking upward. A sound was coming from above, the steady drone of many airplane engines. The sky was full of planes! Abruptly, rows of white puffs appeared beneath the planes, drifting down toward the ground. The world's first major assault by airborne troops was taking place!

For centuries, leaders of armies dreamed of delivering large numbers of troops suddenly and unexpectedly near an enemy army, catching it by surprise and inflicting a crushing defeat. For centuries this couldn't happen. Troops had to come

At 5:30 A.M. on May 10, 1940, German paratroopers landed in the Netherlands and proceeded to capture and guard strategic points in anticipation of the German ground attack. In the background are bridges over the Maas River near Moerdijk.

at their enemy across land—horizontally. The enemy generally had guards watching for an attack, so attackers were sure to be seen long before they could get into position for a surprise assault.

But when a balloon carried two men several hundred feet into the sky in France in 1783, a few generals and others realized this might be a way to make what could be called a vertical attack—attackers coming down on all sides rather than across, horizontally. One person who saw this possibility was the American inventor, scientist, and statesman Benjamin Franklin. How could a country have enough soldiers on guard to prevent several thousand men from coming down out of the sky to make an attack, Franklin asked in a piece he wrote in 1784.

Of course, such a thing wasn't really possible in Franklin's time. Balloons could hold only two or three people and couldn't be steered in any way.

Balloons were new, but the idea of parachutes had been around a long time. In 1495, the Italian artist and inventive genius Leonardo da Vinci made a drawing of one, which he called a "tent roof," and in 1783 French physicist Sebastian Lenormand successfully jumped from a tower. In 1797, a Frenchman named André-Jacques Garnerin made a parachute jump from a balloon over Paris. Once again, military leaders saw the possibility for a vertical envelopment—surrounding an enemy with troops that came down from the sky. But there was still nothing but balloons to carry the troops, and balloons still couldn't be steered.

Then, in 1903, the airplane was invented.

Gradually, airplanes became able to fly faster and farther. They could be steered to go wherever you wanted them to go. Bigger planes were built, which could hold several people. By the late 1920s, planes capable of holding a fairly large number of passengers were commonplace.

The stage was set for "vertical envelopment" to be used in warfare.

where and come out fighting. They were known as Luftlande, or "air-landing" troops.

Student's two parachute regiments were put together to form what was called *Fliegerdivision 7*. The three air-landing regiments became the 22nd Luftlande Division. These two divisions were joined to form the XI Air Corps.

Thus, in 1939, Germany had something no other country had—a full-fledged airborne corps of 13,500 men trained and equipped to attack from the sky!

General Student visits some of his Fliegerdivision 7.

Chapter 2

THE WORLD'S FIRST AIRBORNE ASSAULT

In September 1939, the armies of Nazi Germany invaded Poland, to regain territory Germany had been forced to give up after World War I. Poland was conquered by the German tank divisions and dive-bomber squadrons in less than a month, so quickly that an airborne attack wasn't needed. However, the invasion of Poland had caused Great Britain and France to declare war on Germany. This was the beginning of World War II.

French forces moved into position behind the Maginot Line, France's string of steel and concrete fortresses 250 miles (400 kilometers) long bordering Germany. A small British army came to France to lend assistance. German forces moved into position behind the Westwall, Germany's line of fortresses on its side of the border. But for six months, nothing much happened.

Then, suddenly, Germany struck at Denmark and Norway, countries to its north. Denmark was invaded so that it could be used as a far-forward airfield for bombing raids against Britain. Norway was invaded to gain control of the sea around it, so that essential shipments of iron that Germany was getting from Sweden could be protected from British warship attack.

The Junkers airborne troops transport, JU-52

Denmark surrendered a few hours after receiving a German ultimatum. German infantry landed from ships. There was hardly any fighting.

But in Norway there was heavy fighting from the start, and the invasion of Norway was the first time airborne troops were used in warfare. Oslo, the main port and capital city of Norway, was taken by parachute troops and air-landing troops that had to fight their way in. German transports, the JU52 and the G38, carrying air-landing troops managed to land at the Oslo airfield, capturing it, and parachute troops captured another airfield, enabling more airborne troops to be brought in to both. The entire city was finally in German hands. Britain and France sent help to Norway, and fighting raged, but eventually the British and French had to pull out to defend France, leaving all of Norway occupied by German forces.

Only a few airborne troops played a part in the battle for Norway, but the entire German airborne corps had a major part in the opening moves of Germany's next conquests. In predawn darkness on May 10, 1940, bombers and fighter planes rose up from German airfields all along the border of the Netherlands, Belgium, and France. They roared over the borders, striking airfields, catching Dutch, Belgian, and French planes on the ground and destroying and damaging hundreds of them. They demolished railroad centers so that Allied troops would not be able to move by trains, and destroyed bridges so that troops could not cross rivers.

After them came scores of big JU52 transport planes, heading into the Netherlands, each carrying twelve men of the German 1st Parachute Regiment. This was the start of the world's first major airborne assault, involving thousands of men.

Parachute troops rained down and seized bridges that their army, coming into the Netherlands behind them, needed in order to move through the country. More parachute troops landed around the three main airfields of the Dutch capital city, The Hague, and captured them. Within minutes, transports carrying men of the German 16th Air Landing Regiment were coming down on the airfields, and soon the airborne troops were moving out to capture the city. Still more airborne soldiers parachuted onto an airfield on the outskirts of the city of Rotterdam and fought to hold it until air-landing troops arrived in transports.

German airborne forces invade Rotterdam.

Not everything went smoothly. Of the 450 transport planes bringing airborne soldiers into the Netherlands, 167 were blown apart in the air by anti-aircraft fire, or shot down to crash. Hundreds of parachute troopers were killed or wounded while they were drifting down to earth. In some places, Dutch troops were able to recapture bridges and drive the paratroopers out of the positions they had taken. In The Hague, Dutch troops fought the airborne soldiers to a standstill, preventing the capture of the city.

But the setbacks didn't matter. The soldiers from the sky still held enough bridges and key points that the army coming behind them, with tanks and artillery, was able to quickly move through the Netherlands and wipe out all resistance. The Netherlands was forced to surrender in just four days.

The invasion of Belgium also began with an airborne assault. But this one consisted of only eighty-five men in gliders.

The main route into northern Belgium was blocked by a huge fort called Eben Emael. Before German troops could advance into Belgium, this fort had to be captured. However, a direct attack against it would have been suicidal. Eben Emael bristled with cannons, antitank guns, and machine guns, and there was no way to break in. The German high command decided there was only one way to make the fortress helpless.

In the morning darkness of May 10, eleven German JU52 tow planes came flying low over Eben Emael. Each towed a large glider carrying seven or eight soldiers. The tow ropes holding the gliders were unhooked and the motorless crafts came whispering down on the fort, so silently the soldiers inside didn't know it.

Some gliders landed directly on top of Eben Emael; others came down nearby. The airborne soldiers who rushed out of the gliders were specialists who had trained for months for this special operation. With explosive charges they demolished the fort's gun turrets, making Eben Emael helpless. When the main German army arrived the next day, the fort couldn't stop them. Thus, German forces swept into Belgium. Belgium's little army was steadily pushed back and finally surrendered only eighteen days after the invasion began.

The airborne troops that parachuted and landed in the Netherlands and Belgium had done exactly what military leaders had dreamed of for centuries. They appeared suddenly, took their opponents completely by surprise, and captured vital places needed to help their armies advance. Warfare was no longer two-dimensional, with troops merely moving horizontally back and forth across battlefields. It had become three-dimensional, with troops that could rain down from the skies!

German reinforcements land on Eben Emael, May 10, 1940.

The airborne troops opened up "corridors" into which poured the tanks, cannons, and troops of German armies. These forces swept through the Netherlands and Belgium to meet the armies of France and Great Britain. France's armies were overwhelmed, as Poland's had been, by the "lightning war" tactics of the German tank divisions and dive-bombers, and sur-

Soldiers clear the rubble of the Bank Underground (subway) Station in front of the Royal Exchange in London.

rendered on June 22. In one of the greatest sea-rescue operations in history, most of the British army in France was taken onto ships of every size and capacity and removed back to Britain, to form the core of an army that began preparing for a possible German invasion of the British Isles. Stunned by the effectiveness of the German airborne assaults, British military leaders began doing everything they could think of to prevent the landings of parachute troops and air-landing units that they felt sure were coming.

But the invasion never took place. From July through October there was a period of intense German bombing attacks, known as the Battle of Britain, in an attempt to destroy the British air force, but this did not work. German bombers continued to make nighttime raids on British cities, but the threat of invasion faded away. Hitler had turned his eyes in a different direction, to the east. There, German airborne troops were destined to play another big part.

Chapter 3

THE END OF THE GERMAN AIRBORNE FORCE

Hitler's main goal was actually the conquest of the Soviet Union. He intended to make Germany the main nation of Europe. Now that France had been conquered and Great Britain was barely holding its own, only the Soviet Union stood in the way.

However, to the south of the Soviet Union lay the region of eastern Europe known as the Balkans—the countries of Albania, Bulgaria, Greece, Romania, and Yugoslavia. Before he could send any German armies into the Soviet Union, Hitler had to take steps to prevent an attack being launched out of one of these Balkan nations against his armies. Bulgaria and Romania were German allies, and Albania was occupied by troops of another ally, Italy, but there was possible danger from either Greece or Yugoslavia. Greece was a British ally, and there were 57,000 British troops in Greece to help the Greek army, if necessary. Hitler decided that Greece and Yugoslavia would have to be conquered by German troops.

The attack on both countries began on April 6, 1941. German forces moved out of Austria (then part of Germany) into Yugoslavia; other German forces moved from Bulgaria into

Greece. Yugoslavia was forced to surrender in just eleven days; Greece was conquered in eighteen.

The British army in Greece was in danger of being trapped and captured. But the army commander received word that British ships were coming to the southern coast of Greece, a region called the Peloponnesus, to take the troops away. The Peloponnesus was separated from the rest of Greece by a canal with only one bridge crossing it. The British only had to get across the bridge and then destroy it so that the Germans couldn't follow and catch them before they could get to the ships.

However, Germany had a weapon that could get ahead of the British and cut them off—its airborne units! At dawn on April 27, 1,500 men of the German *Fliegerdivision 7* were dropped at the bridge to capture and hold it until the German tanks could arrive.

But this move was just a little too late. Most British troops were already across, and the British managed to destroy the bridge with cannon fire. Only a few thousand were captured, and some 43,000 reached the ships and were safely taken away.

About 15,000 of these soldiers were taken to the island of Crete, in the Mediterranean Sea, 60 miles (about 100 kilometers) from Greece. Crete was considered part of Greece and had three military airfields and a defense force of 14,000 Greek troops. A few days later, 12,000 more British troops were brought to Crete by ships, giving the island a total force of about 42,000 men to defend it.

This created another problem for Hitler. A British force on Crete was just as dangerous to Germany as if it were in Greece. Crete could be an air base from which British planes could make raids on German troops and could bomb the oil fields in Romania, which were Germany's main source of fuel for its tanks and planes. Obviously, the island would have to be attacked and captured, and the only ways it could be attacked were from the air and from the sea. The Germans didn't have ships suitable for landing a large invasion force from the sea, so the main attack would have to be made by airborne troops.

This was a terribly risky operation. Parachute troops would have to go in first and capture at least one airfield for the air-landing troops to use. But even if the entire parachute division was dropped at once, it would still be heavily outnumbered. If the parachute troops couldn't capture an airport, they would surely be wiped out, and the invasion would fail.

The British and Greek troops on Crete also had worries. They knew they faced an airborne invasion and needed to take measures to defend the airfields, but they also had to defend the beaches, because they believed the main German attack might come from the sea. Thus, the British commander had to spread out his troops to try to cover as many danger points as possible.

The German airborne corps commander, General Student, quickly put together a plan for the invasion. He decided to drop about 2,500 parachute troops on each of the three main air-fields on Crete. Then, 5,000 air-landing troops would come in transport planes to land wherever they could. Seven thousand men would come in from the sea with heavy artillery and sup-plies, in a fleet of about sixty ships that included everything from fishing boats to freighters.

The attack was launched on the morning of May 20. The first airfield hit was the biggest, called Malame. German bombers blasted the areas around the airfield to eliminate as many as they could of the British soldiers who were sure to be there. Soon after, the transport planes came droning overhead, and the parachute troops began their drop.

The paratroopers jumped from an altitude of 400 feet (120 meters), to reach the ground as quickly as possible. They found themselves falling into a torrent of rifle and machine-gun fire! The British and Greek troops had hidden in dugouts during the bombing, and now came out shooting. Many paratroopers

German parachutes land on Crete at Heraklion as a JU52 hit by British anti-aircraft fire goes down in flames.

reached the ground dead, their chutes settling over them like shrouds.

Those who reached the ground alive were in bad shape. Many were wounded. Some had their chutes caught in tree branches and could only hang helplessly, waiting to be shot or captured. Some had broken bones from making hard landings on the rocky ground. Most had only their pistols to fight with until they could find the weapons packets of rifles and ammunition that had been dropped with them. Thus, for a time, they were almost unable to defend themselves, and took heavy losses. By nightfall, of the 2,500 men who had dropped that morning, only about 1,000 were still alive and unwounded.

Things did not go well for the Germans at the attack on the second airfield, either. Many transport planes were shot down by anti-aircraft fire before the men could even get out of them. Those who were able to jump took heavy casualties on the way down.

The attack on the third airfield also went badly. Fifteen of the transports crashed in flames, and hundreds of parachutists were killed as they drifted down. The survivors who reached the ground were attacked at once by British and Greek troops.

Thus, the first day of the invasion was a disaster for the Germans. The *Fliegerdivision 7* had taken terrible casualties, and none of the airfields had been captured.

However, British forces had taken casualties too, and did not know how badly off the Germans were. At the edge of the largest airfield, Malame, was a small hill held by two companies (about 240 men) of British troops. They had lost a number of men, and their machine guns had been knocked out by German attacks. Their commander did not think they could hold out any longer and decided to withdraw. In the morning, when German paratroopers moved forward to make another desperate attack, they discovered the enemy troops were gone. This meant they now actually held the edge of Malame.

Back in Greece, General Student was getting reports on the situation. He decided to risk an all-out assault on Malame. He sent 600 more paratroops and then began sending transports of air-landing troops. Some of these were shot down, and some were blown up by artillery fire as they landed, but enough soldiers landed to link with the paratroopers and make a strong force. Together, they took the airfield, making it safe for more transports to land with more troops.

The German force supposed to come in from the sea was turned back by British warships that sank many of the troopships. But by the third day of the invasion, there were more than 22,000 German troops on Crete, and the British and Greek forces were being forced to withdraw toward the coast. British warships came to pick them up.

German paratroopers escort captured British soldiers.

By the thirtieth of May, ten days after the start of the invasion, 18,000 British troops had been taken off Crete, and the thousands unable to get away were captured. The battle was over, and Crete had been conquered entirely by airborne troops.

So Crete was now in German hands, and, technically, the airborne invasion had been a success. But the loss of men had been much too heavy. One-fourth of the parachute division had been killed or wounded. Hitler felt he could never risk another battle that would have such losses. He decided the ability of airborne troops to surprise an enemy had been lost, and that enemies would now be expecting airborne attacks and would be ready for them. Hitler decreed that the day of airborne troops was over. From now on, with few exceptions, the German airborne divisions would stay on the ground and fight as ordinary foot soldiers.

Chapter 4

THE ALLIES BUILD AN AIRBORNE FORCE

The day of German airborne troops was over. But for the Allies, Great Britain, and America, it was just beginning! Allied military leaders had carefully studied German airborne campaigns and learned from both their successes and their failures. Now the armies of both the United States and Great Britain began to create airborne forces.

As early as the summer of 1940, British military leaders, impressed by what German airborne troops had accomplished in the Netherlands and Belgium that May, began working to form an airborne unit. The British army had some special, hard-hitting, quick-moving infantry units known as commandos. Men of these units were given the first training to jump into combat by parachute. They became the British 1st Parachute Battalion. Other battalions were formed, and in 1941 the British army gathered them all into what was known as the Parachute Regiment. This was a special, all-volunteer fighting unit, and the men were given maroon berets as their official headgear, to distinguish them from the rest of the army.

FIRST PICTURES of BRITAIN'S PARACHUTE TROOPS in TRAINING

HOW THE BRITISH PARACHUTISTS ARE EQUIPPED : One of the first pictures to be taken at the secret R.A.F. Station in Britain, where the Army and Air Force are collaborating in training our newest arm

By late 1941, a complete British airborne division had been formed. It had six Parachute Regiment battalions, organized into two units called parachute brigades; three battalions of glider troops in an air-landing brigade; an air-landing regiment of light cannons; and units of engineers, medical specialists, and others. It was designated as the 1st Airborne Division, and because all the men of the division wore maroon berets, they became known as the "Red Devils."

The first American parachute battalion, designated the 501st, was put together in the fall of 1940. It consisted of 446 men. After the German airborne conquest of Crete, in 1941, three more parachute battalions were formed—the 502d, 503d, and 504th. Like the British airborne units, these American parachute battalions were made up entirely of volunteers.

The men were taught how to use a parachute, how to hold their bodies as they drifted down, and how to land in a way that prevented injury. They learned a standard way of jumping together from an aircraft. When the pilot of the plane decided he was over the area they were to jump into, he switched on a green light inside the plane. This meant "GO." The men all stood up and hooked the end of a line attached to their parachute covers to a cord running overhead. They began to move toward the plane's door, which was open. When their officer, who was first in line, went out the door, each man quickly followed. As they went out, the men would generally yell a kind of battle cry. The line fastened to the overhead cord yanked their parachute cover off, and the parachute unfurled.

America was drawn into the war in December 1941. Several months later, military leaders agreed that two airborne divisions should be created. It was decided to form them out of divisions that already existed, rather than create completely new ones.

One unit selected was the 82d Infantry Division, which had fought in a number of important battles in World War I. At that time, the division was made up of men from all over the United States, so it had been given the nickname "All American." As an ordinary infantry division, the 82d's three regiments were formed of soldiers trained only to fight on the ground. Within a few months, the division was reorganized. One of the regiments was removed and replaced with a parachute regiment formed of three battalions. The other two infantry regiments were made smaller and turned into air-landing units, which would be taken into combat in gliders. The division was now known as the 82d Airborne Division, but it kept the nickname All American.

The other unit selected was the 101st Infantry Division, which had been broken up after World War I and never reorganized. Now, however, the infantry regiment that had been removed from the 82d became the basis of what was designated the 101st Airborne Division. The division's emblem was a dark blue shield bearing the head of an American eagle, and this soon gave the 101st the nickname "Screaming Eagles."

The new American airborne troops, like those of the British and German armies, were regarded as "elite" units—soldiers just a little tougher, harder fighting, and better trained than

General Dwight D. Eisenhower encourages men of the 101st Airborne Division, the "Screaming Eagles."

ordinary infantrymen of the army. Like the British airborne troops with their maroon berets, the Americans were given something to set them apart from the rest of the army. For them, it was boots—calf-high "jump boots," designed to protect their ankles from spraining or breaking when they hit the ground after completing a jump. Any man wearing those boots was instantly recognized as an airborne soldier. They also wore a special cap emblem, a winged parachute.

When 1942 began, Germany and Italy, known as the Axis powers, were virtually in control of all of western Europe. German armies were pushing into Russia, and in North Africa a British army was struggling against Italian and German forces. If the Axis forces could take over North Africa, they would gain control of the Mediterranean Sea.

But on November 7, 1942, American and British forces under the command of American General Dwight D. Eisenhower (who, some years later, was elected thirty-fourth president of the United States) invaded North Africa. These forces pushed eastward to link up with the British Eighth Army. By May 1943, the Allied armies had destroyed the German and Italian forces in Africa.

Allied leaders met to decide what to do next. Italy was the weaker of the two Axis powers, and after long discussions—and some sharp arguments—it was decided that something should be done that posed a threat to Italy. If it looked as though Italy might be invaded, Hitler would have to pull troops out of other places to help defend Italy. This would weaken German forces in the Soviet Union and France.

Italy is shaped like a boot, and just off the "toe" of the boot, across a narrow stretch of water, lies the large island of Sicily, which is part of the Italian nation. In 1942 it contained Italian army airfields and Italian naval ports and was defended by about 230,000 Italian army troops and two German divisions with a total of about 140 tanks. Allied leaders decided an inva-

U.S. airborne forces on their way to a jump

sion of Sicily would be a definite threat to Italy—if it were captured, it could become a stepping-stone for an invasion of Italy. So it was agreed that a gigantic seaborne invasion of Sicily would be made. British and American armies would be taken by ships from the coast of North Africa, across a short stretch of the Mediterranean Sea, and be landed on the beaches of Sicily.

Soon after that decision was made, the men of the 82d Airborne Division were quietly, with as much secrecy as possible, sent across the country by train to a seaport. They were put onto ships and soon found themselves in North Africa. There, they began to train at making nighttime jumps, and to get toughened up for some big event. They didn't know it yet, but the first step in the invasion of Sicily was going to be a nighttime airborne attack, and it would be carried out by the British Red Devils and the All Americans of the 82d.

Chapter 5

THE AIR ASSAULT ON SICILY

The invasion of Sicily was set for the morning of July 10, 1943. The British Eighth Army and American Seventh Army would come in from the sea at two stretches of beach along the coast. But the night before, British and American airborne soldiers would come down on Sicily to help pave the way for the invading troops.

The British troops making the night assault were the 1st Airborne Division's 1st Landing Brigade, 1,200 Red Devils in 144 gliders towed by airplanes. Their mission was to capture and hold a particular bridge. Six large gliders, carrying twenty-eight men each, were to come down on or by the bridge. The other gliders would land around it, and the soldiers would get to it as quickly as possible. With the bridge intact and held by British soldiers, Eighth Army troops could speed over it to the port city of Syracuse and capture it as a vital port for bringing in reinforcements and supplies.

By 8:20 on the night of July 9, all the tow planes and their gliders were in the air, heading for Sicily. But as they neared it, things began to go wrong. A fierce wind was blowing, and the gliders started to jerk and sway. Two towropes broke, and the gliders went wheeling down into the sea—sure death for the men in them. As the planes crossed Sicily's coastline, scores of searchlight beams suddenly stabbed upward, catching the aircraft in bright white light. Streams of bullets poured up from hundreds of machine guns. Anti-aircraft shells began to explode around the aircraft, sending sprays of metal fragments hurtling through the air.

The air was also full of dust swept off the ground by the howling wind. The tow plane pilots simply could not see where they were going, didn't know where they were, and couldn't see the other planes. The flight began to break up, planes going in different directions. In desperation, some pilots told their gliders to separate from them. Some glider pilots did that on their own. Gliders began to sail downward.

Some went into the sea along the coast. About two hundred men were drowned; others managed to swim to shore. Some glider pilots, trying to make landings but unable to see anything, smashed into trees, stone walls, cliffs. Hundreds of men were killed in crash landings.

Of the six gliders supposed to land by the bridge, only one came down near it. The rest never arrived. The twenty-eight men in the glider hurried to the bridge. Most of them had rifles, some had submachine guns, and some formed machine-gun crews. They all carried razor-sharp knives, hand grenades, and extra ammunition. They found the bridge protected by machine guns inside a dome-shaped steel-and-concrete fortification known as a pillbox, which bullets couldn't penetrate. They charged this and demolished it by pushing hand grenades into the openings the machine guns fired through. Shortly, they had control of the bridge.

The bridge had been rigged with explosive devices to blow it up, but these were discovered and ripped loose. During the night, a few other glider troops that had landed safely nearby arrived. But as the sun rose, there were only seventy-three Red Devils holding the bridge.

Waco gliders of the Ninth Air Force Troop Carrier Command have already landed as their Douglas C46 tugs leave.

Italian forces attacked with armored cars and cannons. The Red Devils hung on, fighting as long as they could. Eventually, out of ammunition and with many wounded, they had to surrender. But the Italians didn't have time to put new explosive charges in place and blow up the bridge. British Eighth Army troops reached the bridge and seized it from the Italians. British tanks and trucks full of soldiers began roaring over the bridge toward Syracuse. By nightfall, it was in their hands.

Of 1,200 Red Devils who had set out to take the bridge, fewer than 100 had finally managed to reach it. The whole British airborne unit had taken enormous casualties, but the job had been done.

For the American part of the operation, the 82d Division's 505th Parachute Regiment, three battalions strong, was reinforced with one battalion of the 504th Regiment, a battalion of airborne artillery, and a company of airborne engineers, trained in both rigging up and disarming explosive devices. This came to about 3,400 men.

The Americans were to parachute at midnight to the beach area where the American 7th Army was coming in the next morning. It would be the 82d's job to hold off enemy troops as long as possible, enabling the 7th Army forces to gain a strong foothold on the shore and begin pushing forward.

About 8:00 on the night of July 9, the paratroopers began climbing into the planes that would take them to Sicily. Each trooper carried a Garand M-1 rifle, which could be fired eight times or in a single burst. Each man also carried 156 rounds of ammunition, a knife, several hand grenades, some food packets, a small compass, and a folding entrenching shovel 27 inches (69 centimeters) long fastened to his belt, with a water bottle (canteen) next to it. Some men carried bazookas, tube-like weapons firing a missile that could penetrate tank armor.

("Bazooka" came from the name a popular American comedian had given an amusing musical instrument he made from metal tubing and a funnel.)

At 8:35, groups of planes began taking off. As each group reached the coast of Sicily, pilots began peering for landmarks they had been told to head for. But they had run into the same murky dust as the British tow plane pilots, and most of them couldn't make out anything. Anti-aircraft and machine-gun fire were pouring up from the ground. Rather than risk having paratroopers killed before they even left the plane, pilots began turning on the green light for the men to jump.

Some planes were blown apart by anti-aircraft fire before the parachutists could even leave them. Some men were hit by machine-gun bullets while still in the air. The heavy wind made parachutes drift long distances before reaching the ground. Instead of all coming down in the area where American troops were going to come in from the sea, the paratroopers became scattered along the coast, often miles from one another.

But gradually, some men located others, and small groups managed to form. They began to do whatever they could to cause trouble for enemy soldiers. Lurking at roadsides, they shot up any German or Italian vehicle that came up the road. They blew up bridges that Italian or German troops might use to get to the beaches. They cut telephone wires, so enemy commanders wouldn't be able to issue orders to distant units. Encountering machine-gun positions, they sneaked as close as they could, then fired rifles and threw grenades. They knocked out pillboxes by shoving grenades through the openings, or blew them open with bazookas.

One group of about ninety All Americans captured a farmhouse that had been fortified by Italian troops with barbed wire strung around it and pillboxes in front. From prisoners they took, the Americans learned that a German panzer (tank) divi-

A captured pillbox

sion was on its way. When the panzer division arrived, the paratroopers, using the farmhouse's fortifications, fought off attacks by German infantry and demolished two tanks with bazookas. They eventually had to pull out of the farmhouse and retreat, but they had prevented the panzer division—thousands of men and about one hundred tanks—from reaching the beach and possibly turning the American landing into a bloodbath.

Actually, both the British and American airborne assaults had gone badly wrong. Nevertheless, the American and British armies that came ashore on July 10 had an easier time because of what their airborne troops had accomplished. They were able to push forward quickly and head inland. By August 17, the Italian and German troops had evacuated Sicily, and the island was in Allied hands. Despite terrible losses and the breakdown of their plans, the All American paratroops and Red Devil glider troops had helped make victory possible.

Chapter 6

INTO EUROPE

With the capture of Sicily, Allied commanders began preparing for an invasion of Italy.

In 1943, Italy was technically a kingdom. However, the king had no real power, and the country was actually ruled by a man named Benito Mussolini, who had the title *Il Duce*, "The Leader." Like Adolf Hitler, Mussolini was a dictator, and he controlled every part of Italian life. But by 1943 most Italians were sick of the war they had been in for six years, and of their lack of freedom. When Sicily was captured, Italian military leaders secretly contacted the Allied leaders without Mussolini's knowledge. An agreement was made that Italy would drop out of the war and that the Italian army would not become involved in any fighting when the Allies invaded. Of course, this was a tremendous benefit to the Allies, for it greatly reduced the numbers they would have to fight against.

It did not mean there would not be any fighting, however. Italy was full of German troops, and the German commanders

Hitler and Mussolini at the Tomb of the Fascist Martyrs in Florence, Italy

were determined to do everything they could to prevent Allied forces from moving up through Italy into Germany.

The Allied invasion of Italy began on September 8, 1943. Airborne troops were not used before or during the troop landings. But on September 13 and 14, 2,100 paratroopers of the 82d Airborne Division and 640 men of the 509th Parachute Regiment were dropped to provide instant reinforcements for the American troops that were in danger of being pushed into the sea by a ferocious German attack.

The 82d's drop was a success, with almost all the troopers coming down exactly where they were supposed to. But the 509th Regiment's drop was a near disaster. The men were dropped in an area into which German troops had come. More than a hundred Americans were killed or captured. The others did what they could to blow up some bridges, cut phone lines, and wipe out small groups of German soldiers. Then they cleared out and headed for the American lines.

The battle for Italy was long and savage. There were no other Allied airborne operations, but there was one very small but astonishing one by the Germans. When Italy dropped out of the war, Benito Mussolini was arrested by Italian generals loyal to the king, and imprisoned in a small hotel in the mountains of central Italy. But Hitler could not let his "partner" suffer such indignity.

On the morning of Sunday, September 12, ninety German airborne troopers landed around the hotel in gliders. They rescued Mussolini from his astounded guards. He was flown to safety in northern Italy, which was in German hands. There, he became a figurehead leader of the part of Italy under German control. But when German forces finally pulled out of the region, withdrawing before an unstoppable Allied advance, Mussolini was left on his own. He was captured by Italian "partisan" soldiers who were aiding the Allies. They shot him and hung his body up by the heels in the market square of the city of Milan.

Even while the battle for Italy was going on, preparations began for D Day—what would be the greatest seaborne invasion in history—an assault into France, which was occupied by more than 750,000 German troops manning a line of menacing fortifications running all along the coast.

Should large-scale airborne assaults, such as by whole divisions, be part of the invasion? This was one of the things considered early on. Most British commanders believed so, but some American military leaders were firmly against it. One of them was General Eisenhower himself.

So many things had gone wrong with airborne operations in Sicily and in Italy, so many men had been lost, that it seemed as if perhaps large airborne assaults by whole divisions were too dangerous and wasteful to risk.

Then something happened to change everyone's mind. The United States was fighting a major war in the Pacific region, against Japan, as well as in Europe. On September 5, a parachute regiment in the Pacific was dropped on the coast of New Guinea, to help block the retreat of Japanese forces in the face of an invasion by Australian troops. The drop was perfect in every detail.

American generals who had become suspicious of the effectiveness of airborne troops decided that they could be effective after all. It was agreed that American airborne divisions could be used in the invasion of France.

The final plan for the invasion included three airborne divisions. By this time, the British army had formed a new airborne division, the 6th. This would be one of the parachute and glider divisions to invade France. The other two would be the American 82d and 101st Airborne Divisions. Again, as in Italy, the airborne forces would go in at night.

However, lessons had been learned from Italy, and it was agreed that before airborne units went into action again, some changes had to be made. There had to be a way to make sure that pilots of planes carrying paratroopers or towing gliders could easily find the places where the troops were supposed to land. Airborne commanders decided that "pathfinders" would have to be used—groups of troopers dropped in advance of the main force, to mark the places where paratroopers should be dropped and glider troops should be cut loose. Men from the 82d and 101st Airborne Divisions were selected to go to "pathfinder" schools to learn how to do these things.

Following the success of the airborne liberation of New Guinea, the United States began the long and costly process of liberating the rest of the Pacific islands from Japanese forces. Paratroopers land on Numfoor to capture Japanese airfields in this photograph from 1944.

By the beginning of June 1944, everything was ready. Britain was packed with troops, trucks, tanks, and planes. Hundreds of ships crowded its harbors. The greatest invasion in history was about to be launched.

The region of France selected by Allied generals for the invasion was Normandy, on the northwest coast. It was determined that the Normandy invasion had to be made on either the fifth, sixth, or seventh of June, to take advantage of a full moon and low tides on those days.

But as June began, the weather turned bad. Storms made visibility poor and turned the sea rough. It looked as if the invasion would have to be postponed, which could ruin its chance of success. German spies would undoubtedly learn all about it.

Then, meteorologists reported that one of the three days might have good enough weather to risk making the invasion. It was a gamble that General Eisenhower had to take. "Okay," he told his staff officers. "We'll go." The day set for the invasion to begin—D Day—was the sixth of June.

The top commanders of the German army were expecting Allied forces to attempt an invasion of France. They knew the best time in June for that invasion would be the fifth, sixth, and seventh of the month. So, when the weather turned bad, most of them felt sure the invasion attempt wouldn't be made in June. In any event, they didn't think it would be made in the Normandy region, because that was farthest from the coast of England, with the longest water crossing. Most of them felt that the Allies would pick a much nearer place to attack.

However, even though they didn't think it would be attacked, they made sure the Normandy region was fortified and well defended. Explosive mines and steel-girder obstacles were placed underwater all along the beaches, to blow open the bottoms of landing boats or to snag them so they couldn't reach the beach. Pillboxes and heavy gun emplacements, with barbed

The German defenses along the French coast in Normandy: British Pioneer soldiers are detonating them to facilitate the landing of the Allied forces seen on the horizon.

wire strung in front of them, overlooked the beaches. The Germans even had special defenses against airborne attacks. Open fields that looked like good places for paratroops to land were filled with buried land mines that could blow a man's leg off if he stepped on one. Low-lying fields near rivers were flooded so paratroopers would sink into them and drown. In places where gliders might land, the Germans embedded row upon row of wooden poles, a foot thick and 8 to 12 feet (2.5 to 3.5 meters) high, for the gliders to smash into.

So, on the night of June 5, 1944, German forces in France waited and wondered when and where the invasion would strike. As the night went on, heavy Allied bombing raids hit targets throughout Normandy. From England, some 176,000 Allied troops began to move across the English Channel, in a fleet of more than 4,000 landing crafts and warships. Ahead of them went the airborne infantry.

Chapter 7

AIRBORNE FORCES IN THE INVASION OF FRANCE

The first Allied soldiers into France were the pathfinder teams, the paratroopers trained to go in first, find their way to the areas where the paratroops and gliders were to land, and guide them in. To do this, they were equipped with devices called Eureka radar-radio beacons, which sent out a powerful signal that pilots of tow planes and transports could follow regardless of weather or other factors. The pathfinders also had electric lights that projected an intensely powerful beam easily seen by the incoming pilots.

Most of the pathfinders were loaded down with as much as 100 pounds (45 kilograms) of equipment! For fighting, they carried a rifle, generally four grenades hooked to their parachute harness, and a knife strapped to a leg. Some had bandoliers (ammunition belts) with as many as three hundred cartridges in them, slung around their necks. Their entrenching shovel and water bottle were fastened to their belts. In their pockets were chocolate rations, a smoke grenade or two, an antitank mine or two, and a squeezable container full of morphine attached to a hypodermic needle, called a syrette, in case they were injured and needed something to relieve the pain.

The American pathfinders and all other American paratroopers also carried one very special item of equipment, a small toylike metal noisemaker called a cricket, which when squeezed gave two sharp loud clicks. This was a recognition signal for men moving in darkness.

If a soldier thought he saw other soldiers, he was to give two clicks, and if he heard two clicks come back, he knew the others were Americans.

British pathfinders had smudged their faces with charcoal so their skin wouldn't gleam in the darkness. Most of the Americans, however, had painted their faces with designs in red, green, black, and white, as Native American warriors going into battle once had done. Many Americans also had their hair cut like Mohawk warriors of hundreds of years before, with most of the head shaved, and only a strip of hair running down the middle.

The pathfinder planes began taking off about thirty minutes after sunset, at about the same time the troop-landing ships began sailing toward France. Most of the planes were over France and dropping their pathfinders shortly after midnight. Many of the men were under machine-gun fire on the way down. Some were killed, and some landed wounded, able only to lie in pain, wondering what would happen to them.

As quickly as they could, team members freed themselves of their chutes and loose equipment, located each other with clicks, turned on their lights, and began to send out radio signals for the paratroop and glider planes now winging their way toward France.

At about the same time the pathfinders were making their drops, a small force of British 6th Airborne glider troops was coming in to carry out a special mission. They were to capture two bridges controlling major roads. Control of these bridges

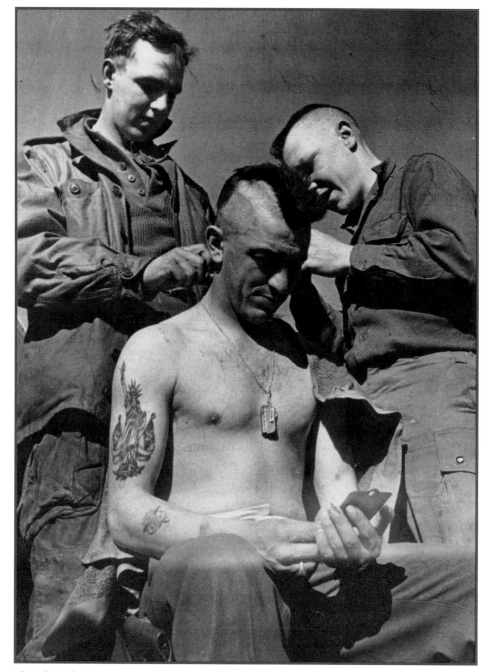

An American paratrooper gets a Mohawk.

would prevent German tank units from being able to attack the flank of the British troops that would land on the beaches.

The tow planes crossed the coast of Normandy at 12:07 A.M., June 6, and the gliders dropped off, their pilots guiding their crafts toward the target area. At 12:15 the pilot of the leading glider spotted two lines of silvery water running side by side a few hundred yards apart. One was the river Orne, the other the Caen Canal. A road ran straight through both of them, and where the road crossed each, were bridges. The gliders were to land between the bridges, and the soldiers were instantly to attack each bridge and capture it before it could be blown up by its defenders.

The first glider touched ground heading straight for the canal bridge, which was fortified and blocked with barbed wire. The glider slammed into the wire at about 60 miles (97 kilometers) an hour and was stopped short with a sudden jarring impact that momentarily knocked every man unconscious. Seconds later, they regained their wits and rushed from the glider, heading to the bridge.

The second glider came down a minute later. It broke in two, but no one was injured, and the men hurried to go to the aid of the first platoon. The third glider crash-landed behind the second, and one man was killed and a dozen pinned in the wreckage. Those who could rushed to the bridge.

The German soldiers defending the canal bridge were caught completely by surprise. A few were killed, but most ran away or surrendered. By 12:22, the British controlled the canal bridge.

The other three gliders contained the platoons that were to capture the river bridge. Two came down several hundred yards away, but the third landed 7 miles (11 kilometers) away, in the wrong place. The first platoon to reach the bridge found that the German troops guarding it had apparently run away. So, the river bridge, too, was under the 6th Airborne's control.

By now, the rest of the airborne forces were arriving. Thirteen thousand men of the U.S. 82d and 101st Division, in 900 airplanes, were coming down in a 50-square-mile (130-square-kilometer) region beyond the beaches where the American seaborne forces would land. About 3,000 others were coming in gliders. Eight thousand troopers of two British 6th Airborne Parachute Brigades were dropping in the areas where British forces would come in from the sea.

Planes were also dropping thousands of realistic rubber models of paratroopers, fastened to real parachutes. These were rigged with small firecracker-style explosives that went off as the dummies came down, making it sound as if they were firing weapons. The dummies caused the Germans a lot of concern, for they made it seem as if more paratroopers were coming down than actually were.

At around 1:00 A.M., parachute troops of the 82d Airborne Division's 505th Regiment drifted down into the countryside outside a town called Ste. Mère Église, a few miles from the coast. A railroad track and highway ran through Ste. Mère Église, which made the tiny town a major target. The 82d Airborne troopers were to assemble outside the town, move in, and capture it.

But about thirty paratroopers came down directly in the heart of the town. An Allied bomber had accidentally dropped an incendiary (fire-starting) bomb on the town, and a house was afire. Many townspeople were out fighting the blaze, and some sixty German soldiers were watching them. Now, hearing the sound of the American planes overhead, everyone looked up and beheld white parachutes drifting down toward them. The Germans began firing into the sky. Many of the Americans were killed or wounded in the air. A few drifted helplessly down into the blazing building, to burn alive. The parachutes of some men became snagged on tree branches, telephone poles, and

Allied forces attacking German positions in France, June 6, 1944

projecting parts of buildings. They hung there until they were captured—or shot.

Meanwhile, about one hundred paratroopers had landed outside the town, gathered together, and were headed toward Ste. Mère Église to carry out their mission. Entering the town, they quickly got into close combat with the German troops there. By 4:30 A.M. they were in control, and Ste. Mère Église became the first French community to be liberated from the Germans.

By now, German officers in various parts of Normandy were getting reports of captured towns and bridges and heavy fighting, and began to dispatch troops to find out what was going on. At about 1:30, two German tanks came rumbling toward the canal bridge held by the British 6th Airborne glider troops. The British soldiers destroyed one with a rocket-propelled missile weapon known as a Piat, similar to an American bazooka. The other tank retreated. Soon after this, the men at the bridge were reinforced by a battalion of para-troopers.

Thus, as the sun rose, there were 17,000 airborne troops in Normandy, holding bridges, towns, and roads, to prevent the Germans from moving tanks and troops to the beaches where the Allies would be landing in a few hours.

However, this was done at terrible cost. Despite the efforts of the pathfinders, the air landings were nearly as disastrous as they had been on Sicily. Many paratroop units were dropped far from where they should have been, sometimes coming down in places thick with German troops, where they were quickly cap-tured or killed. Hundreds of men of the 101st Airborne were wiped out by being dropped in flooded fields, where the heavily laden paratroopers simply sank in and drowned. Dozens of gliders smashed headlong into the rows of wooden poles, killing or injuring everyone in them.

But despite these dreadful disasters and losses, most of the missions had been carried out successfully. Once again, air-borne troops had paved the way, this time for the greatest inva-sion in history!

Chapter 8

ASSAULT BY AN AIRBORNE ARMY

The seaborne invasion of Normandy on June 6 was relatively easy in some places, horribly bloody in others. But gradually, Allied forces were able to move forward, and more troops and equipment came in behind them. By the beginning of July there were about a million men and 150,000 vehicles pressing ahead, steadily driving German forces back.

In August, the Allies suddenly struck again. Another invasion force, formed of American and French troops, sailed up from Italy, most of which was now in Allied hands, and landed in the south of France. This was done to keep German forces there from moving up to attack the Allied armies in northern France. The invasion of the south was preceded by a drop of airborne troops.

The airborne force was put together from airborne units that had been left in Italy when the others went to Britain to take part in the D Day invasion. There were three British and two American parachute battalions, an American glider battalion, two American airborne artillery battalions, and a few

The Siegfried Line consisted of concrete antitank barriers and deep trenches. Sections of it were camouflaged.

smaller units. These 9,742 men took off from Italian airfields in the morning darkness of August 15, in 535 troop carrier planes and 465 towed gliders. Their job was to seize a number of towns and block any German advance toward the beach, so that the troops coming in from the sea could gain a strong foothold. There was a thick fog over the French coast, and the airborne troops got spread over a much wider area than had been intended. Even so, they managed to carry out their mission, and the invasion was successful.

By August 30, Allied troops had advanced nearly to the German border. Before them lay the Siegfried Line, or Westwall, Germany's line of fortifications running along the border. When they broke through that, they would be invading Germany. But suddenly, the advance was halted. The Allied supply line was now stretched so far that the troops facing Germany had to stop and wait for supplies, fuel, and ammunition to reach them.

This was a bad situation. It would take a long time for the Allied troops facing the Westwall to build up enough supplies to resume their advance, and that would give German forces time to build up their strength. Something had to be done quickly to keep the Allied advance going.

British Field Marshal Sir Bernard Montgomery, commander of the Allied 21st Army Group, suggested an astonishing plan—an assault by an entire army of airborne troops! Montgomery urged putting down a "carpet" of airborne soldiers through a strip of the Netherlands along the German border 64 miles (103 kilometers) long. If these soldiers could capture a number of bridges controlling a main road into a part of Germany beyond the end of the Westwall, Allied armored divisions could simply thunder across the bridges onto German soil, going around the Westwall instead of through it.

It was a daring and dangerous plan. The entire area the airborne troops would land in was occupied by German forces. If anything went wrong, the airborne army might well be wiped out. When Montgomery explained the plan to General Eisenhower, the supreme commander, Eisenhower told him, "Monty, you're nuts!"

The Allies had the airborne army to carry out Montgomery's plan. It was made up of the U.S. 82d and 101st Airborne Division, the British 1st Airborne Division, and the

(Left to right) American Lieutenant General Omar Bradley, British General Bernard Montgomery, and British Lieutenant General Miles Dempsey

Independent Polish Parachute Brigade, formed of Polish troops who had managed to get to Britain after their country had been conquered. This huge force had been labeled the First Allied Airborne Army.

Despite Eisenhower's astonishment at Montgomery's plan, he eventually okayed it. If it worked, it could almost certainly end the war.

But German commanders knew an attack was coming, and they hurriedly built up their defenses. They didn't know where the assault would hit, but strengthened their forces as much as possible all along the border. Some of the last German panzer divisions available were brought forward to the border, and troops were scraped up to fill out the German infantry divisions.

The Allied attack, which was labeled "Operation Market Garden," began on the night of September 16, with enormous bombing raids on German airfields and anti-aircraft gun positions in the area where airborne troops would come down. Unlike the airborne assaults on Sicily and Normandy, "Market Garden" was to be a daylight assault. At 9:45 A.M., 2,023 troop transports and glider tow planes began taking off from twenty-four airfields all over England. They carried some 35,000 men.

Germany no longer had enough fighter planes to try to stop this huge air armada. By about 12:30 the planes were roaring into the skies over the Netherlands, and the first drops began.

The U.S. 101st Airborne was dropped farthest south. Its job was to seize several bridges over canals and rivers within the first 15 miles (24 kilometers) of the "carpet." The paratroops captured the first bridge easily, then ran into strong opposition from German forces in the area. Fighting their way to the town of Son, they found the bridge there had been blown up by the Germans. Quickly engineers constructed a narrow, flimsy bridge that enabled the airborne soldiers to keep moving. By the next day, they reached the town of Eindhoven, which they were to hold until the arrival of a British armored division coming from Belgium.

Some 12 miles (19 kilometers) farther north, 7,227 men of the U.S. 82d Airborne came down around the city of Nijmegen, Belgium. They were to capture a main bridge in Nijmegen and several others in nearby towns, as well as to seize a stretch of high ground that controlled the area. Fighting their way forward, they captured two of the bridges. But reaching Nijmegen, they found trouble. Part of a German panzer division, with tanks and heavy artillery, was in the city.

Men of the 82d managed to seize control of one end of the Nijmegen bridge and hold it. On September 20, they crossed the river in canvas assault boats, under heavy fire, and captured the other end. With the British armored division entering the city, the German panzer division troops pulled out.

Paratroops and glider troops of the British 1st Airborne Division came down farthest north, near the Dutch city of Arnhem. They were to capture an important bridge that crossed the Rhine River running through the city. The Polish Parachute Brigade was dropped near them, to help.

But there were a German panzer division and other German units in Arnhem. The Red Devils seized one end of the bridge but then found themselves in a fight for their lives, against tremendous odds, as German troops began to surround them. By September 25 they had lost about 1,570 men killed and wounded, and some 6,000 taken prisoner. The remaining 2,400 Red Devils and their Polish allies were forced to make a stealthy escape, leaving the Arnhem bridge in German hands.

Thus, the Allies had taken only a narrow strip of Dutch territory and were still unable to advance into Germany. The Allied losses in Operation Market Garden were more than 17,000 men; German forces lost only about 10,000. The German army was still intact and well able to keep fighting.

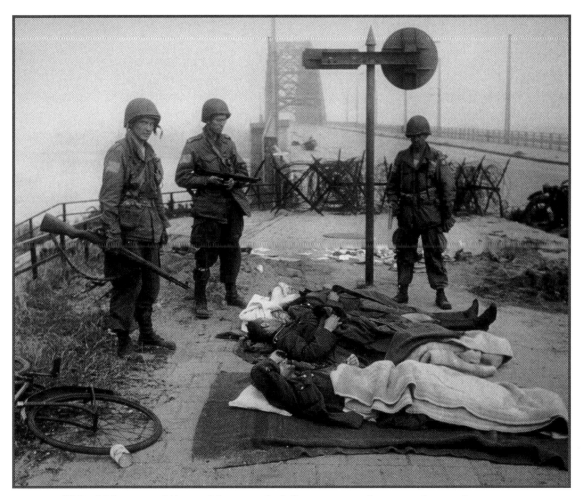

U.S. Airborne soldiers with wounded German captives stand guard at Nijmegen Bridge, Netherlands.

By early 1945, some Allied troops finally penetrated into Germany, but in the north, the whole 21st Army Group was blocked at the Rhine River. Allied military leaders put together a plan for a combined crossing of the river by troops in boats and airborne troops.

German soldiers (shown) have captured or killed British paratroopers who were dropped into an impossible situation near Arnhem.

At midmorning on March 23, 21,680 soldiers of the British 6th Airborne Division and the new U.S. 17th Airborne Division came down by parachute and glider beyond the Rhine near the German town of Wesel. By midafternoon they had captured all their objectives and taken some 3,600 prisoners. Troops and supplies came pouring across the river in boats, and the operation was a complete success. It was the last airborne operation in Europe. On May 8, Germany surrendered, and the war in Europe came to an end.

There were only a few airborne operations in the Pacific area during the rest of World War II. In 1944, a division of Indian troops of the British army landed in Burma in gliders and transport planes. And in 1945, another new U.S. airborne division, the 11th, made drops and landings during the American invasion of the Japanese-held Philippine Islands. On September 2, 1945, Japan officially surrendered, and World War II was over.

After World War II, there were some parachute troop drops in the Korean War (1950–1953), the Arab-Israeli wars (1948–1973), and the Vietnam War (1957–1975), Grenada (1983), and Panama (1989). The weapon of airborne infantry developed in World War II has a new form. There are still airborne divisions, but they now reach their targets in helicopters and giant troop transport planes.

There will probably never again be any huge drops of thousands of paratroopers and glider troops as there were in the Netherlands; on Crete, Sicily, and Normandy; and for Operation Market Garden.

Index